First Facts®

ALL ABOUT MEDIA

WHAT'S YOUR SOURCE?

USING SOURCES IN YOUR WRITING

BY BRIEN J. JENNINGS

CAPSTONE PRESS
a capstone imprint

First Facts Books are published by Capstone Press,
1710 Roe Crest Drive, North Mankato, Minnesota 56003
www.mycapstone.com

Library of Congress Cataloging-in-Publication Data is available on the Library of Congress website.
ISBN 978-1-5435-0220-6 (library binding)
ISBN 978-1-5435-0224-4 (paperback)
ISBN 978-1-5435-0228-2 (ebook pdf)

Editorial Credits:
Erika L. Shores, editor; Juliette Peters, designer;
Morgan Walters, media researcher; Kathy McColley, production specialist

Photo Credits:
Alamy: Sean Prior, 21; Capstone Studio: Karon Dubke, bottom 17, middle 17; Shutterstock: Artur. B, (icons) design element, David Osborn, (penguin) Cover, imtmphoto, (girls) Cover, Maksim Kabakou, bottom 11, mattomedia Werbeagentur, 15, Orange Line Media, 13, Rawpixel.com, 5, 7, top 11, Shahrul Azman, 19, Supphachai Salaeman, design element throughout, Tonis Pan, (computer) Cover, Tyler Olson, 9, Vladimir Volodin, 12, wavebreakmedia, 17

Printed and bound in the USA.
122017 010999R

Table of Contents

A Research Project

Your class is in the library to **research** deserts. You will write a report to share what you find. Where do you look for information? You will have to find sources.

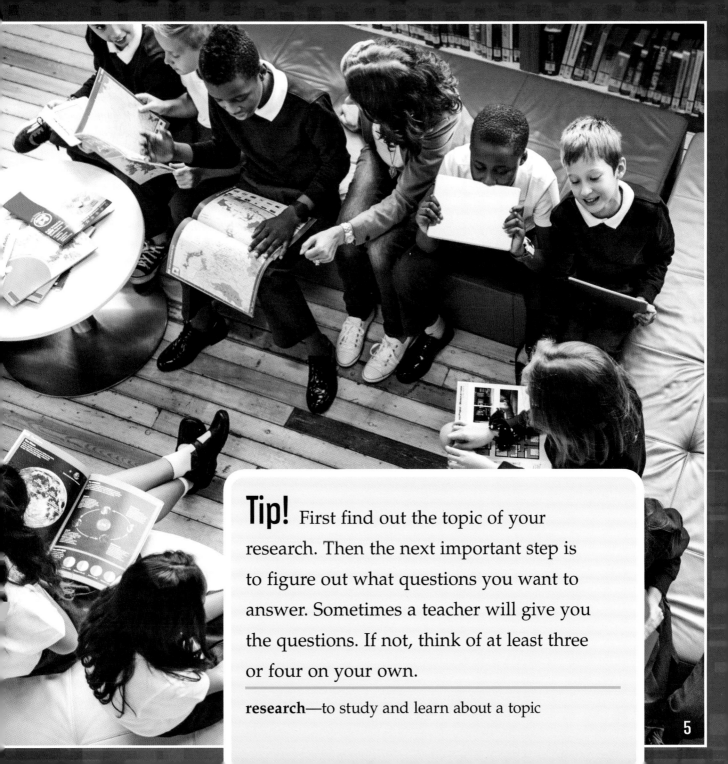

Tip! First find out the topic of your research. Then the next important step is to figure out what questions you want to answer. Sometimes a teacher will give you the questions. If not, think of at least three or four on your own.

research—to study and learn about a topic

All About Sources

A library is full of sources. Books, newspapers, websites, and videos are common sources. A librarian can help you find the right source for information on your topic.

> **TIP!** Encyclopedias can be great sources to get started with research. Most encyclopedias are online and easy to search. Encyclopedias give facts on many different topics.

Many researchers start by looking in **nonfiction** books. Nonfiction books have facts. Facts can be proven true. People who write nonfiction books check to make sure what they are writing is **accurate**. Nonfiction writers do not include their own ideas or **opinions**.

Books shouldn't be your only source for information. You need to get information from many sources.

accurate—exactly correct

nonfiction—written works about real people, places, objects, or events

opinion—a way of thinking about something, not a fact

The Internet makes it easy to find information. Anyone can go online almost anywhere and find almost anything. You need to be careful to make sure the information you find online is true. Look for websites made by museums, colleges, and news organizations. People who work for these places make sure the information they put on their websites is true.

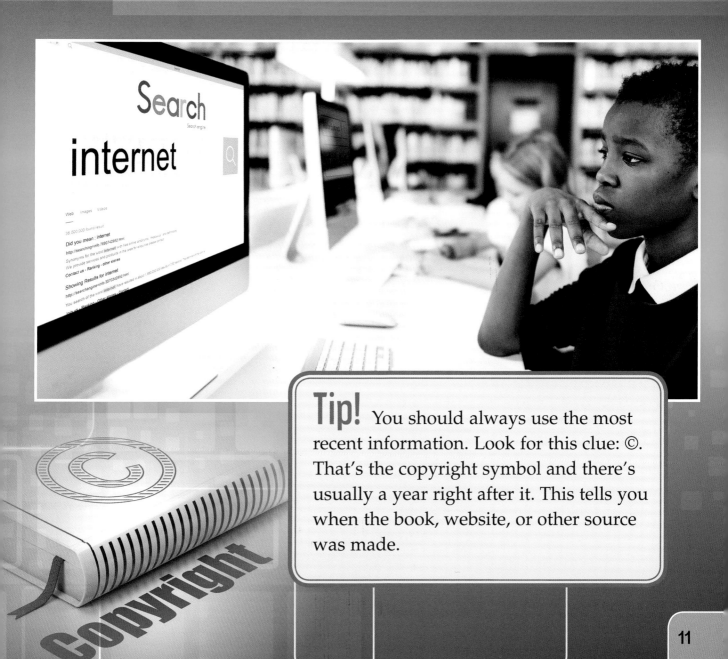

Tip! You should always use the most recent information. Look for this clue: ©. That's the copyright symbol and there's usually a year right after it. This tells you when the book, website, or other source was made.

Go Right to the Source

Using **primary** sources in your research is a great idea. Photos and letters are primary sources. Diaries and **interviews** are primary sources too. They are made by people who have firsthand experience of an event. People wrote down their experiences or took photos.

primary—first

interview—a meeting to ask someone questions to find out more about something

TRY IT! Ask a relative to tell you about something they experienced firsthand. Record the interview on a camera or smartphone. Your interview is a great example of a primary source.

Choosing Sources

With so many sources to choose from, picking the right ones is an important step in research. Ask some questions to find out whether a source is useful. First, is there enough information, and is it easy to understand? Is the source **trustworthy**? Can you find the author and **publisher** information? Does the source contain facts or opinions?

TIP! If you are unsure about what source to use, ask a librarian or teacher. Librarians and teachers know what makes a good source.

publisher—a person or company who makes media available to the public

trustworthy—something you can believe

Copyright and Plagiarism

The copyright symbol does more than let you know how old a source is. It also lets people know that someone owns the information. Authors, photographers, and other creators own their work. They must get credit for it.

Deserts are *ecosystems*.
These areas are dry and get little rain. Most deserts are very hot, but some are cold. Some deserts even get snow. Some deserts are sandy, while others are rocky.

First Facts are published by Capstone Press.
1710 Roe Crest Drive, North Mankato, Minnesota 56003
www.mycapstone.com

Library of Congress Cataloging-in-Publication Data
Cataloging-in-publication information is on file with the Library of Congress.
ISBN 978-1-5157-6886-9 (library binding)
ISBN 978-1-5157-6892-0 (paperback)
ISBN 978-1-5157-6904-0 (eBook PDF)

Editorial Credits
Anna Butzer, editor; Heidi Thompson, designer; Morgan Walters, media researcher;
Kathy McColley, production specialist

Photo Credits
All photos shot by Capstone Studio, Karon Dubke; Shutterstock: amgun, Cover, design element throughout, FRDMR, left 18, greenazya, 21, Robyn Mackenzie, right 18

TABLE OF CONTENTS

When writing a report, you should not copy words directly from sources. Using other people's words as your own is called **plagiarism**. It is the same as stealing someone else's work.

TIP! Don't copy word for word. Only write the most important words. These are called keywords. Make sure to write down where you find your information.

plagiarism—using someone else's words, pictures, sounds, or ideas without permission or giving them credit

You've found the best sources. You gathered the information. You made a list of the titles and authors of your sources. Now it's time to write your research report.

Be an information detective to find and use the best sources.

Ask yourself these questions:
- How new is the information?
- Does your source have information you can use?
- Can you tell who created the information? Who is the author or publisher?
- If your source is a book, is it full of facts or opinions?
- If it is a website, are there ads? Is the website trying to sell you something? If it is, you might not trust it.

Glossary

accurate (AK-yuh-ruht)—exactly correct

firsthand (FURST-hand)—straight from the source, original

interview (IN-tur-vyoo)—a meeting to ask someone questions to find out more about something

keyword (KEE-wurd)—an important word

nonfiction (NON-fik-shuhn)—written works about real people, places, objects, or events

opinion (uh-PIN-yuhn)—a way of thinking about something, not a fact

plagiarism (PLAY-juh-riz-uhm)—using someone else's words, pictures, sounds, or ideas without permission or giving them credit

primary (PRYE-mair-ee)—first

publisher (PUHB-lish-er)—a person or company that makes media available to the public

research (REE-surch)—to study and learn about a topic

trustworthy (trusht-wur-THEE)—something you can believe in

Read More

Clapper, Nikki Bruno. *Learning About Primary Sources.* Media Literacy for Kids. North Mankato, Minn.: Capstone Press, 2016.

Howell, Sara. *How to Gather Information, Take Notes, and Sort Evidence.* Core Writing Skills. New York: PowerKids Press, 2014.

Owings, Lisa. *Do Your Research.* Library Smarts. Minneapolis: Lerner Publications Company, 2014.

Internet Sites

Use FactHound to find Internet sites related to this book:

Visit *www.facthound.com*

Just type in 9781543502206 and go.

Check out projects, games and lots more at
www.capstonekids.com

Critical Thinking Questions

1. What is one way you can decide if a source is trustworthy?

2. What does plagiarism mean?

3. Describe why primary sources are good to use in your research.

Index